How to Make Your Science Project Scientific

How to Make Your Science Project Scientific

Revised Edition

Tom Moorman

John Wiley & Sons, Inc.

Published by John Wiley & Sons, Inc., New York
Published simultaneously in Canada
Design and production by Navta Associates, Inc.

The publisher and the author have made every reasonable effort to ensure that the experiments and activities in the book are safe when conducted as instructed but assume no responsibility for any damage caused or sustained while performing the experiments or activities in this book. Parents, guardians, and/or teachers should supervise young readers who undertake the experiments and activities in this book.

Library of Congress Cataloging-in-Publication Data is available from the publisher.

ISBN 0-471-41920-6 (paper)

Printed in the United States of America

10 9 8 7 6 5 4 3 2 1

CONTENTS

PREFACE

A science project can and should be good science. Too often, however, exhibits at science fairs are examples of "bad" science. Although the students and teachers involved are probably trying to do good science, they may be unsure about the rules of scientific methods and practices.

How to Make Your Science Project Scientific shows the student how to do "good" science, the way the professionals do it. This doesn't mean that doing science right requires costly laboratory equipment or an advanced education. It simply means following guidelines, described in this book, that are based on standards that have been agreed upon by professional scientists.

This book can be especially useful to students and mentors of students who are doing science projects. But its true goal is to help anyone better understand how science works and how it can benefit everyday living.

CHAPTER 1

What Is Scientific?

Most people know little about the methods of science. Yet, without these methods, the results of scientific work are meaningless. How do we know that the results are accurate and reliable if we do not know what methods have been used to find out those results? Take the question, "Are dogs more intelligent than hogs?" Most people would reply, "Dogs are." But what methods did they use to find this answer? Dogs are regarded by humans as friendly, cute, and loyal, and they are kept close as pets. Hogs and pigs

are considered dirty, to be raised mainly for food. Because many people like to be around dogs more than pigs, they make the assumption that dogs are smarter than pigs, but they never test this assumption.

Observation ◄————————————————————

Method of observation is the key to learning the real answer to such a question. How do you go about making fair observations? How do you make observations in which your biases have little effect on the results? When you can be reasonably sure that your methods of investigation are going to help guarantee honest results—results not seriously affected by prejudgment you may have made—then you may say you are being scientific. Controlling the prejudice problem is a key difference between ordinary, "commonsense" knowledge and scientific knowledge.

If you work on a science project and want it to be really scientific, you must be sharply aware, at every step, of your own prejudice about the outcome. This doesn't mean that having a prejudice is altogether wrong, or that it should keep you from doing a particular project. Let's say you like dogs and really don't know anything about the intelligence of pigs and hogs. Okay, so you have a prejudice. You'd like to find out that dogs are more intelligent than pigs. How can you test the intelligence of both kinds of animals without letting your prejudice affect the results? Once you plan a fair method for doing that, you are getting scientific about it.

But science is more than just planning how to get an answer to a question. It is more than using your reasoning or your logic. Science means the actual observation of things, of events, of phenomena. You can't be scientific until you actually do some observing of your subject. Observing, of course, means more than just seeing. It means using all of your senses as well as your measuring instruments, such as rulers, meter sticks, balances, clocks, and thermometers. It means using instruments that amplify the stimuli that your senses receive, such as telescopes, microscopes, sound amplifiers, and oscilloscopes. It means using recording equipment of many kinds (beside pencil or pen), such as cameras and tape recorders.

Keeping Records ◄─────────────────────────

An important part of being scientific is keeping records because it helps you to report to others accurately and honestly about your observations. Record keeping helps people to check up on you, and the knowledge that others will check up on you helps to keep you from letting your prejudices affect your results.

Being Objective ◄─────────────────────

"Objective" is the word we use to mean keeping our prejudices or biases under control. Being objective means that your findings are not shaped by your feelings or prejudices but by direct observation. It means that others who make similar observations will find that they can agree with you, even though they may have different feelings or prejudices about the results of the investigation. When observers can agree on the results, in spite of their varying prejudices, the results can be called objective. This, then, is why your records are important and why you must plan to report to others on both your *methods* and your *results*.

Being Selective ◄─────────────────────

How can we be sure that the things we choose to know, choose to learn, are a good, a true, and a valid selection of all the possible things there are to know? All of our past experiences come to bear on this choosing and this valuing. Our experiences with other people also help to determine our attitudes and values. In addition, experiences related by other people bring us new things to learn. However, some of the knowledge we get from others is valuable and some of it is not. How do we decide which is which?

A living human being has countless experiences every moment. Some experiences take place within ourselves, and others involve ourselves and the surrounding environment. But we cannot possibly notice, observe, or report on all of these experiences, even though they may be changing us in many subtle ways. One cannot notice every heartbeat, every leaf falling, every mosquito buzzing, every drop of rain. And so we select the things we will notice or observe about our-selves or our environment.

Thus, because we make selections, we find that we observe our sur-roundings with bias or prejudice. What you select to observe, another person may completely miss. Or what you fail to observe one time you may closely study another time.

What's Wrong with Common Sense?

The name for the things people claim to know, true or not, as a result of ordinary, widespread experience is common sense. We must use this term carefully. It has two widely different meanings: (1) A person who makes careful judgments based on sound information is said to use common sense. (2) Any ideas or concepts that are widely accepted by many people but that have not been carefully tested for their truth-fulness are also called common sense (or common knowledge).

Common sense, for example, might suggest that heavy things fall faster than light things. Many people accept this statement as true, although a little careful thought should show that it is not a good statement, even without scientific testing.

There are many other commonsense ideas—some good, no doubt, and some not so good—and all of them needing testing. Why can't we just accept commonsense principles as okay?

The problem with taking a casual or commonsense approach to the example of whether heavy things fall faster than light things is that there are too many variables. What do we mean by too many variables? In our example you can see that people observe "light" things, such as feathers, dead leaves, and inflated balloons, as falling rather slowly. And people observe "heavy" things, such as rocks, metal tools, and chunks of wood, as falling rather fast. So they conclude, "Heavy things fall faster than light things." Scientists would say that these people have not noticed that there are two or more variables confounding the results.

The following experiments can help us test the commonsense prin-ciple that heavy things fall faster than light things. They will show how size (or area) is an important variable.

A toy balloon, when inflated, is light of weight and, yes, it falls slowly. If compared to a rock, we must agree that the rock falls faster than the balloon. But we can see two main differences or variables: (1) difference in weight and (2) difference in size or area. We can take a balloon and easily arrange for an experiment with one variable only— size or area. We simply use the same balloon for both trials, first inflated, then deflated, in each trial dropping the balloon from the same height. In doing so, we observe that the balloon inflated (larger area) falls more slowly than the balloon deflated (smaller area), even though their weights are about the same.

We can make an even better experiment if we use two balloons of the same shape and size, one inflated, one deflated, and drop them side by side at the same time from the same height.

We can plan another experiment with balloons in which size or area is the same and weight is the variable. Use two balloons of the same size and shape. Make one heavier than the other by putting a weight into it, for example, a penny. Inflate the two balloons to as nearly the same size as possible and drop them from the same height, taking care to release them at precisely the same time. We see that the heavier balloon does fall faster. Now we have one experiment that does not support the commonsense principle and one that does.

A third experiment is needed, using an inflated balloon and a piece of metal, for example, a paper clip, that is lighter than the balloon. Drop the inflated balloon and the paper clip from the same height at the same time and observe the results. In this case, the lighter object (the paper clip) falls faster than the heavier object (the balloon). So, by conducting three rather simple experiments we have observed all of the following:

A. Two things of the same weight falling at different speeds

B. A heavier thing falling faster than a light thing

C. A lighter thing falling faster than a heavy thing

As a result of this conflicting evidence, we could conclude that something is wrong with the commonsense statement that heavy things fall faster than light things. This statement is too simple to cover the varying results of our three experiments.

One might go further by experimenting with objects that are heavier than balloons, as Galileo, the great seventeenth-century Italian scientist, is thought to have done. An example would be to compare the falling speeds of two wooden balls of the same size and shape but of different weights with one ball hollowed out and filled with lead. Also, one might use more complicated equipment to create a space without air (a vacuum space) and arrange for two objects to be dropped at the same time, one with a vacuum space, to compare their falling speeds.

After enough good experimenting and observing, one might finally make a statement that would correctly express the falling speeds of things light and heavy, large and small, in air and in vacuum. We see, however, that when many variables are present all at once, as in ordinary observation, the results are what scientists call "confounded." They are mixed up too much for the simple, commonsense statement to be accurate.

Not only are there too many variables for truthful results in much common observation but also there is often too much chanciness. For example, common explanations for catching a cold are: "I got my feet wet" or: "I sat in a draft and got chilled." These explanations have been shown through careful testing to be unreliable causes of colds. However, people may get their feet wet or get chilled by a draft at just the "right" time for it to seem that one of these events caused a cold. This kind of chance happening of events at certain times and places often seems to confirm a commonsense principle, even though better testing may show the principle to be wrong.

It will not do, however, to say that all commonsense principles are wrong. Many have a grain of truth, although it may not be clear which are the truthful parts and which are not until someone performs tests good enough to be called scientific.

Anecdotal Evidence ◄─────────────

Another kind of evidence to take a closer look at is often called **anecdotal evidence.** Sometimes a person brings to a discussion a story out of his or her personal experience as evidence to support a proposition. Such a story (or anecdote) may seem very convincing to the person telling the story and to his or her listeners. Nevertheless, as evidence, the anecdote may have all of the weaknesses of common sense. The events described in the anecdote may have happened suddenly, without plan, and the person telling about the events may have had only a narrow, prejudiced view of what happened.

But suppose a person is honest and accurate in giving the anecdotal evidence. Suppose, let's say, that a man took vitamin "Z" all winter and did not have a single cold, while people all around him had the usual colds. Are we going to accept this anecdote as evidence that vitamin Z prevents colds? Not likely. There is a chance that the man might have gone through the colds season without catching a cold, even if he had not taken the vitamin. It takes a broader and more thorough investigation of this sort of situation before we can conclude that we have established a good general principle. And so   we must be wary about accepting anecdotal evidence because of its chanciness as well as the possible prejudiced nature of the observations.

There is a place, of course, for what is called naturalistic observation, the study of people and things under natural conditions. But one must have a plan for how to make the observations objective and the results reliable. We will consider these methods further in the next chapter, "Scientific Methods."

CHAPTER 2

Scientific Methods

You do many experiments every day; each of us does. When you try a different soft drink to find out if you like it, that is an experiment. If you talk to another person to try to learn if you want to become better acquainted, that's an experiment. How is a science experiment different from the countless other experiments you do?

Causality

Let's be sure that we understand what we mean by the word "experiment." Usually it means changing something to learn what happens because of the change. In experimenting, we are trying to understand how some things that happen cause other things to happen. That is very important in science. It is the study of what a scientist calls **causality** or a **cause-effect relationship.**

As we grow up, causality is one of the most important things we learn—how to make something happen by doing something else that causes it. Babies do not understand anything about the language of the people around them, but they soon learn that crying gets attention from others. That is the beginning of the baby's learning about causality.

Experimentation ◄————————————

Scientists do their experimenting with a more formal plan. A scientific experiment usually contains these steps or stages:

1. Identifying a **problem**
2. Stating a **hypothesis** or a proposed solution to the problem
3. Stating a **procedure** or a plan that may help you find a solution to the problem
4. **Performing the experiment,** or carrying through the planned procedure
5. **Recording data,** or making any other records that may be used in reporting the experiment
6. **Publishing a report** so that others may check up on your experiment and perhaps repeat it

Problem and Hypothesis ◄————————

As you plan your project, state as clearly as you can the question or problem you will investigate. Do this in writing. Then write out a description of the method you plan to use. As you plan method and materials, you will see more clearly how to express your hypothesis. This should state as clearly and precisely as you can what it is that you expect to prove or disprove.

Example A

Question: Does nitrogen help to make corn grow better?

Hypothesis: Sweet corn planted in sandy loam in planters in the laboratory and treated with 2 grams of urea per liter of water will show a significant increase in height at two weeks after germination as compared with a control planting.

Example B

Question: Can mice grow normally if they are fed only dried peas?

Hypothesis: White mice born in a cage and fed only whole dried peas will make normal growth to age 60 days as compared with a control group fed Brand *K* mouse food.

Hopefully your hypothesis can be stated definitely so that it can honestly be tested. But proven? No. (See chapter 13 for more about proof.)

Investigation ◄──────────────────

Experimentation is a very important scientific method, but it isn't the only one. There are several other important scientific methods, however, and we need to refer to them by a term other than the word "experiment." Scientists most commonly use the words **investigation** and **study** for these other methods.

An example of the need for methods other than experimenting is the belief in astrology. Many people believe that the positions of the planets in our solar system at the time of a person's birth cause the person to behave in certain ways. Is Nathan a person who gets angry easily because he was born when the planets were in certain places? Of course there is no way to do an experiment with the planets to test such a belief. Other kinds of science investigations are better tools for testing astrology.

One problem with the experimenting we do in ordinary living is coincidence. Sarah's long-time friend surprised her one day by visiting her unannounced. However, Sarah said that she knew her friend was coming for a visit because Sarah had dreamed about her visit the night before. Did her dream "foretell" the visit? Or was it just a coincidence? Would Sarah have forgotten about the dream if the friend had not come?

Because countless things happen at the same time only by coincidence, an important goal of a science investigator is to try to spot real cause-effect relationships and to separate them from coincidence.

Reporting ◄──────────────────

As discussed in chapter 1, reporting is a crucial requirement in doing a science investigation. You must *publish a report* of your investigation. Displaying your investigation in a science fair is an important way to "publish" it. That means that you must keep very good records of your investigation at every step along the way so that you can report to others in a way that they can repeat your investigation and reach the same results. In science, that system is called **replicating** an experiment or investigation. That someone else can achieve the same results is at the heart of doing science. This replicating by others is what makes scientific information so reliable. If the same procedure consistently produces the same results, then we know that something more than mere chance is at work.

The following chapters will introduce you in more detail to the science methods mentioned here, as well as many more.

CHAPTER 3

Simple Experiments

In science, the term "simple experiment" has a specific meaning. To understand the differences between a simple experiment and a more complicated, controlled experiment, consider this example. Suppose that you are watching a candle flame and ask yourself, "Would the color of the flame be different if I added salt to the pool of melted wax at the base of the flame?" If you do this to only one candle, it is called a simple experiment. You can make it a better experiment, a controlled experiment, by using two candles of the same type. You light both, then add salt to the wax of one but not to the other.

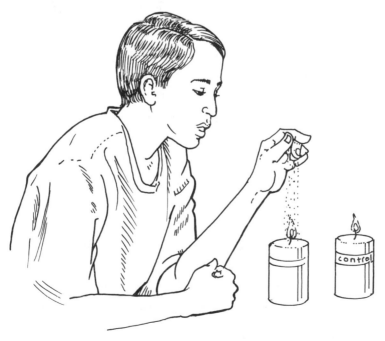

13

After you have made your experimental change, you can now compare the two candles side by side. In the next chapter you will see how and why such controlled experiments can be much better science than simple experiments.

Experimental Terms ←———————————————

There are some special terms that will help us talk about different kinds of experiments:

▼ **Experimenter**   (that's you)

▼ **Independent variable**   The thing you are changing, in this case the salt you are adding to the wax of one candle. You, as the experimenter, make this change.

▼ **Dependent variable**   The effect of the change, in this case how the color of the flame changed after you put the salt in the wax of one candle. This change *depends upon* the independent variable.

▼ **Result**   Your observation of the change. In this case, what you observed about the change in color of the flame

If the flame does change color when you add the salt to the wax, we say that the independent variable and the dependent variable are **related variables.**

As an experimenter, you must try not to let other things change beside your two main variables. Let's say that you want to learn whether adding baking soda to the water used for watering bean plants will make them grow better. You must decide how much baking soda to put in the water and carefully observe the growth of the plants before and after giving them this water. Obviously, you must not make any other changes, such as adding more water, using different temperatures, or using a different amount of light. These variables would **confound the results;** you would not be able to judge which of the four variables—baking soda, or more water, or different light, or different temperature—might be related to any difference in growth. So you try to keep other possible variables **constant,** or the same, during the experiment. You try to keep all possible variables constant except the one you built into your experiment—adding the baking soda to the water as your independent variable.

Experimental Design ◄──────────

Scientists use the term **experimental design,** or **design of the experiment** (or other investigation) to refer to different kinds of experiments. The design of the investigation is a most important part of doing good science. Professional scientists are always faced with the problems of the costs of an investigation, the amount of time they can devote to it, and other limits. You surely will be faced with similar limits as you do your investigation.

Many science projects displayed at science fairs cannot be seen as good investigations because the students simply did not put enough thought into their design. For example, you might see a project on growing plants that displays just one plant in each of two cups of soil. The experimenter's intention was to compare two different factors in the growth of the plants, such as a fertilizer ingredient or the color of the light. The big mistake in such limited investigations is the notion that the differences between just two such plants would be meaningful.

PLANTS
LOVE MY
FAVORITE
SODA !

The fact is, the plants will differ anyway; no two plants are exactly alike. Therefore, the results are probably meaningless. The student doing such an investigation should consider investing much more thought, time, and materials in the project.

How many plants, or people, or animals should there be in such an investigation? For now, consider that 25 or more specimens should be used in each part of a controlled experiment for the results to be meaningful. Deciding about such numbers will get us into the study of what is called statistics. To some people, that term is a scary one, but it should not be. You are using statistics when you compare the scores of two teams in basketball, football, or other sports. You are using statistics when you look around a schoolroom and determine that there are more girls in the class than there are boys. You are using statistics when you judge that, at a certain age, girls on the average are taller than boys. Statistics simply means collecting and analyzing numerical data.

Statistics are a very important part of living as well as doing science, and you should learn how to be friendly with statistical concepts.

CHAPTER 4

Controlled Experiments

In experimenting, the term **control** has special meaning. Here's an example of a very simple controlled experiment about making lemonade. Start with two glasses containing the same amounts of water. Into the first glass, put one teaspoonful each of sugar and lemon juice. Into the second glass, put two teaspoonfuls of each. The first

glass is called the "control," and the second glass is called the "experimental." By tasting one and then the other, you can make a better judgment about the changes than had you used only one mixture. You can continue to change the amounts of sugar and lemon juice in the experimental glass while the control glass stays the same.

Growing Popcorn Plants ←

An experiment with growing popcorn plants can demonstrate a more advanced controlled experimental design. It requires more materials, equipment, and time, but it can be made much more meaningful:

Use two identical planters with the same kind of soil in each one. Plant 30 popcorn seeds in each planter. To water the experimental planter, you will add baking soda to the water in carefully measured amounts, such as one level teaspoon of baking soda for each quart of water. To water the control planter, you will use plain tap water. Use the same amounts of water in each planter. Try to keep all other conditions—for example, temperature and light—the same for both planters.

In setting up a controlled experiment, many decisions must be made. For example, which seeds will you use for the experimental and which seeds for the control planter? You will take all of the seeds from the same package, of course. Of course? There, you see, is an important decision. You want the seeds to be as much alike as you can get them— as alike in inherited traits as possible. As you pick the seeds you should be careful to choose uniform, sound seeds (e.g., not broken, undersized, or discolored). See appendix A for instructions on how to do a seed germination test to make sure the seeds you have are viable.

Even with all this care, it is possible for prejudice to begin to affect results, so do not decide yet which planter will be experimental and which will be control. You will use a **random choice** method for making this decision, as you will in making others to come. Put the two groups of seeds into separate containers, then decide which group goes in which planter by random choice, "blind," as in taking names out of a hat or in tossing a coin.

At this point, some people might say. "Why all this bother? Why not just plant the seeds and get on with it?" Of course, if one were just planting seeds for the fun of it, or for growing food, you would not worry about doing it by random choice, in an unprejudiced manner. We must look ahead, however, to the final judgment—your report—that will depend very much on the making of random decisions at this early stage, and when you report your findings, you want to have full confidence in your methods.

Continue to make as many decisions as you can randomly: The soil you use in each planter must be mixed thoroughly in one large container and then transferred alternately to each container in small amounts so as to not favor either. Plant the seeds by spreading them in as nearly the same pattern around each planter as you can, and take care to cover them uniformly with soil.

Now you are ready to choose which planter is to be the control and which is to be the experimental. To make an unprejudiced decision, a random choice, you might flip a coin.

The rule is to arrange to make as many random decisions as you can—by tossing a coin, pulling numbers or names out of a hat, using a list of random digits, or by other means. Even though you held constant as many variables as you could, there are probably unknown variables that you could not make constant, for example, differences in

the genetic traits of the seeds, or differences in the soil about which you may not know. Therefore, you will need to take your chances on these unknown variables. They may work for or against your hoped-for result—your hypothesis.

Can we ever make the conditions exactly alike in the two parts of a controlled experiment—aside from the independent variable? Not likely. Nevertheless, we can count on a controlled experiment to give more valid results than a simple, uncontrolled experiment would give us, and certainly more than the usual mixed-up conditions of ordinary, everyday life.

Measuring Results ◄

When the plants have grown to a point that you feel you can judge the results, you end the experiment. Carefully measure the heights of the plants in each planter to compare them, keeping careful records of the measurements for each planter. If a camera is available, take photographs, always with the planters marked in such a way that it is easy to see in the photo which one is experimental and which one is control.

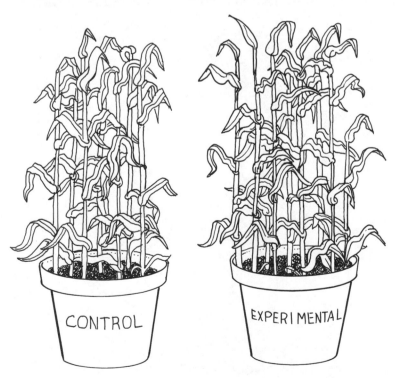

An even better way to measure the plants for comparison is to weigh each one on a laboratory balance scale. Dig up each plant, taking care not to damage the roots. Carefully wash the soil off of the roots and lay out each plant on newspaper to dry, keeping the plants for each planter separate while you do the washing and drying. Next, weigh each plant and carefully record the weights for the experimental and for the control.

Now the statistics: For each planter, calculate an average, or mean, of the weights (or measure the lengths if you did not use a balance). You can now compare the averages to determine whether the independent variable—the baking soda in the water—made a difference in the growth of the plants.

Here a most important problem comes up. We can assume that the mean weights of the plants in each planter will differ somewhat, anyway. So how much difference do you need to show to be able to claim that the baking soda in the water (the independent variable) made a *significant* difference? Of course, if the plants all died in the experimental planter, you have no problem. Most often, however, the differences are not that obvious. In this case you need to use statistical methods for deciding how much difference is meaningful or signifi-cant. The term **significant difference** should become part of your thinking about any investigation you do.

CHAPTER 5

Counterbalancing Controlled Experiments

Y ou want to settle an argument among friends about the following question: Does loss of sleep reduce a person's physical strength? You decide to test this hypothesis: Sleeping only four hours in a night instead of eight hours will increase the time it takes a person to run 100 meters the following day. Working with people is much more complicated than working with plants or animals, but let's see how it might work as an example of **counterbalancing.**

Determining the Effect of Loss of Sleep on Physical Strength ◄────

You will need eight friends who agree to work with you; they are the subjects of your experiment. It would be better if all the subjects were of the same sex and close to the same age. Sex and age should be constants, as nearly as you can make them.

Your independent variable will be the differences in the amount of time your subjects have spent sleeping the night before they do the test run. Your dependent variable will be the time it takes each person to run 100 meters. You will need a stopwatch and note-taking materials.

For the first night, randomly divide your subjects into two groups. Group 1: All four subjects will sleep eight hours. They will go to bed at 10:30 P.M. and get up at 6:30 A.M. Group 2: All four subjects will sleep only four hours. They will go to bed at 2:30 A.M. and get up at 6:30 A.M.

We are assuming for this example that all have agreed to run 100 meters out at the school athletic field, and to do their best running against a stopwatch.

The next morning, as soon as you can, get all of your subjects together at the school athletic field. With your stopwatch ready, have each person do a 100-meter run and record the time for each. Their running times are the dependent variable in this experiment.

Now for the counterbalancing part of this experimental design (also called the cross-over design): On the second night, the Group 1 subjects (who got eight hours sleep the night before) **sleep only four hours.** The Group 2 subjects **sleep eight hours.** (See table 5.1.)

TABLE 5.1 COUNTERBALANCING PLAN		
Trials	Control Group (8 Hours of Sleep)	Experimental Group (4 Hours of Sleep)
Trial 1 (first day)	Group 1	Group 2
Trial 2 (second day)	Group 2	Group 1

When all the running trials are finished, compute the average, or mean, timings of all eight runs for each of the eight-hour sleepers and for each of the four-hour sleepers. Then try to determine if there is a meaningful difference. In this experiment, counterbalancing is used to take care of differences that may already exist between the two groups. It would be practically impossible to find two groups of people who are nearly matched in running ability and other characteristics. Therefore, if you want to make a fair test using only a controlled experiment, you need a counterbalancing plan as well.

This running experiment shows how the counterbalancing principle can help to "wash out" differences among experimental subjects. There is no way, obviously, to wash out all of the differences among the eight people in this example.

It would be hard to do such a counterbalancing plan in many controlled experiments, even ones with simple subjects like popcorn plants. The problem there would be that, once you have done an experiment with one variable, for example, a fertilizer additive, you cannot switch the subjects so as to get a fair test.

When to Use Counterbalanced Experiments ◄——————————————

A simple experiment, neither uncontrolled nor counterbalanced, may be good enough for testing a hypothesis about fairly simple physical things. But for experiments in biology and in the ways people and animals behave it is difficult to hold constants steady so that only the variables change. For these experiments we need better experimental plans—controlled experiments with counterbalancing.

Will this pet mouse eat this dried pea? A simple, uncontrolled experiment will serve: The mouse eats the pea or it does not.

Can mice live healthfully on dried peas? Now things are not so simple, and you would want a controlled experiment: a control group that is fed a good normal diet and an experimental group (as evenly matched as possible with the control group) that is fed only dried peas.

Is there more fighting among mice living in crowded conditions than in conditions that are less crowded? Here it is better to use a counterbalanced plan. You would need carefully matched groups in two cages or pens, one cage or pen large enough for the number of mice and the other cage small and cramped. Keep everything else constant—food, water, litter, ages, sex, light, and temperature. After a few days of observing and recording of any aggressive behavior in each group, switch each group to the other cage and observe again for an equal amount of time.

The experiment with people that tests the effects of loss of sleep on running speed has the problem of prejudice, especially on the part of the subjects. You, the experimenter, are aware of the prejudice problems. How about the subjects of the experiment, the ones doing the sleeping and running? Do they have prejudices about the hypothesis? Surely some of them would have. And, if so, how would their prejudices affect the results? Some of them might run harder after the short sleep just to show that they were "tough," or because they don't believe their running speed will be affected by a little loss of sleep. Others might be prejudiced in the opposite way. This prejudice among human subjects is a difficult problem. Professional scientists often deal with such prejudices by using experimental designs called "blind" and "double-blind," which we describe in the next chapter.

CHAPTER 6

Blind and Double-blind Experiments

The experimental design called **blind experiment** is used most often when the subjects in the experiment are people. Sometimes the subjects know too much about the experiment or are biased. Therefore, the experimenter must work out a way to keep them "blind" about the independent variable, that is, without foreknowing what has changed. Here is an example that illustrates the place that blind experiments hold in science investigations.

Blind Experiments ◄

Jack enjoys experimenting with cookery, changing recipes to learn how to make some of the foods he prepares taste better. On the grocery store shelf he finds a box of pure cocoa with no sweeteners or other additives. He asks himself, How would chocolate cookies made with that pure cocoa compare with cookies made with the baking chocolate I always use? He finds in a cookbook a formula for substituting cocoa for baking chocolate, and he bakes two batches of cookies. He refers to those with cocoa as "A" and those with baking chocolate as "B."

Jack invites a group of friends over and offers the cookies, which he has separated into two cookie jars, one labeled "A" and the other

labeled "B." He explains to them that, without knowing the difference, or while "blind" to the difference, they are to try each kind of cookie and tell him which they prefer.

The blind experiment is much used by scientists who are investigating painkillers, dietary additives, and other variables. Blind experiments are used when it is important that the subjects do not know or are "blind" to which treatment they are getting, if any. That way the subjects can be completely honest about the effects of their treatment. In such experiments, the scientists often will give one group of subjects a "dummy" or **placebo** pill, one that does not contain any of the medicine being tested. The subjects, of course, are not told which they are getting—the active medicine or the placebo. Even then there is often a problem because the subjects in a blind experiment sometimes convince themselves that they are getting the active medicine, and their belief tends to affect them as if they were actually getting the medicine.

An investigator can avoid this problem by using the following approach: the investigator makes up two different painkillers or analgesics in identical forms such as tablets or capsules, and issues them to subjects with pain problems without telling them which kind of pill they are getting. Then, as the subjects report back about the results of the two painkillers (or analgesics), the investigator can make a decision about their effectiveness.

For your own investigations, you might consider blind experiments in the area of cookery, as with Jack's experiment with cocoa. Or, you might want to try comparing the effects of coffee, with or without caffeine, on performance in mathematics, such as memorizing digits, on athletic performance, and so on. You might find other ways for using blind experiments. The prejudice problem on the part of experimental subjects tends to demand it.

Double-Blind Experiments ←

To be doubly sure that the results of an investigation are not influenced by the prejudice of the investigator, scientists rely on the **double-blind experiment.** Suppose, for example, a scientist has been much involved in the research on a treatment for the common cold, one that relieves symptoms and actually hastens recovery. Let's say scientist Blackmore has total faith in her new cold remedy and very much wants to see her discovery go over in a big way. The problem is this: How can Blackmore do her experimenting and be totally honest about the results, not kidding herself or anyone else? To do this, she uses a double-blind experimental design.

First, she gets someone she trusts to make up some pills in two batches, one that contains the new treatment for colds and the other one a placebo. Next, she recruits a suitable number of people to take part in the experiment. They are told that they will be randomly assigned to the experimental or to the control group by the tossing of a coin or by taking names out of a hat. The subjects are blind to which group they will be in.

Now, here is where the double-blind factor enters. Blackmore herself does not know which group each subject is in. She gets her trusted associate to give out the pills to each subject, and neither the subjects nor Blackmore knows who receives which one.

After enough time has passed for the subjects to have colds and to use their pills, Blackmore interviews each subject. She questions them about the effectiveness of their treatments and summarizes the effectiveness of each in a report. When she is finished, Blackmore's associate shows her which subjects received the new treatment and which subjects received the placebo pills. Only then can Blackmore and others honestly judge the effectiveness of her cold treatment.

This use of a double-blind experimental design is complex and costly. Even so, it is a very important form of experimenting, and it has great advantages when both subjects and experimenter know too much about the goals of the experiment.

Case Studies

When you are limited to one example in your investigation, it is called a **case study.** Often this is the best you can do. A medical doctor, for example, must work with a patient on that patient's individual problem, called a **case.** If you choose to make the study of a single fish in an aquarium, or a single bean plant, your science investigation would be called a case study. A case study can be a proper form of science, even though there are often advantages in observing larger numbers of cases or specimens.

Investigating a Single Specimen

For now, let's say that you are limiting your science investigation to a single specimen or case. You should set your goal as finding out everything you can about your single specimen, be it a bean plant, a mouse, a moth or butterfly, or an elephant. You should also expect to make a good scientific report of your study.

To keep our example fairly simple, let's say that you choose to make a study of a bean plant. A single bean plant is a very complicated thing. If you were to try to take it apart and study every detail of its makeup, you could spend a long time at it. You should have access to a good microscope and plan to use it. This in itself demands a lot of expert technique. You should find a good book on the making of microscope slides and do some practicing before you get going on your real specimen. You then examine leaf sections (or cross sections), stem sections, root sections, and the many different surfaces of the plant. Describe what you find in as much detail as you can. Also, try to get a plant in the blooming stage and describe the blossoms in good detail. In addition to verbal descriptions, you should plan on making some sketches, even if your drawing skills are not very good.

You may decide to try making photographs of the specimen through the microscope. This is another very demanding technique. You must mount the camera on the microscope, decide on proper exposure of the film, and so forth. You may need help from someone who has experience in such work.

Investigating a Group

A study of the behavior of a group of people can also be a case study. You may want to make a science investigation of all of the new kids in your school at the beginning of a school year, or of the people in a church choir, or some other group. In such studies, you may generalize about the people in various ways.

Anthropology and sociology are sciences that focus on large groups of people. Anthropologists try to investigate people in parts of the world that have been little changed by modern civilization. These subjects are sometimes called "indigenous" people, or "preliterate," or "oral," meaning they do not have a written language. Such a study would also be called a case study. Sociologists usually work at observing people in larger groups, perhaps even whole countries or nations.

Generalizing ◂────────────────────

As these examples show, a case study is the investigation of a single specimen or group, even though the results of such work may lead to generalizing. You generalize when you say something like, "All dogs bark at strangers" or, "People are just naturally selfish." You, as a worker in science, should be careful about such generalizations. We will see later what the very practical problems are in making generalizations from a limited number of specimens that you may observe.

CHAPTER 8

Naturalistic Observation

The term **nature study** is used in the sciences mainly for the observation of plants and animals in their natural settings. There is an obvious problem: How do you find something (plant or animal) in its "natural" condition? Humans have spread out over our planet Earth (and into space) and have changed conditions so much that we have made it hard to find things in their natural settings. You can study planets, stars, and galaxies in their natural conditions because there is nothing we can do to change them. Such a study is clearly naturalistic observation. While you cannot experiment with the stars, constellations, or planets, you can observe them and report on what you observe.

Studying Animals and Plants

Bird watching can be a good kind of naturalistic observation, even in and around big cities. Many people find observing birds fascinating. There appears to be great variety in the way birds get along in their settings—what they feed upon, their nesting habits, their mating habits, their plumage, and so on.

If you live in or near the country, there are many opportunities in fields, woods, and streams for naturalistic observation. An important limit in such observations is to try to observe the plants or animals in ways that do not disturb them as they go about their natural ways. In

contrast with experimenting, you try **not to change** the object of your investigation.

On what kinds of plants does a wild rabbit feed? How many baby rabbits does a wild female rabbit have at one birthing? How often does she bear young? In what seasons of the year? How many of the young live long enough to mature and to reproduce? What other animals such as foxes and hawks prey on rabbits?

Finding answers to such questions is all part of doing naturalistic observation for a science project. This kind of observation can be a good way to do science, and it has been the result of much of what we know about the world around us. Can it be done in a city or town? Yes,

but there it is sometimes harder to find plants and animals in their natural conditions. Trying to observe insects or angleworms (earthworms) in a natural setting could be a fairly good project, assuming the area has not been sprayed with insecticides or is not too heavily fertilized. Or, if you do attempt such a study, you might want to include the weed killer or fertilizer as part of the "natural" conditions under which the worms or insects now exist.

Why do naturalistic observation? As early European explorers went around the world, they discovered a great many species of plants and animals that they had not seen before. They gathered specimens and put them on display in zoos and museums to enable many other people to understand about the great variety of species in existence. Always, there were questions about how and why all of this great variety came to be. Scientists make much of trying to answer such questions, as we will explore later in the themes of **cause** or **causality.**

These days it is especially hard to find people in natural settings for observation. Yes, anthropologists work at doing this, but far from big cities and other "modern" places. You may ask, Isn't it "natural" by now for people to live in big cities? In a way, that's right. Humans are moving into different ways of living, but we are still part of nature.

As these examples show, it is still possible to do naturalistic observation scientifically. However, it takes a lot of skill and determination to find and observe suitable subjects. As in any scientific investigation, record-keeping is important in naturalistic observation. Methods include note-taking, sketching, still photography, videotape, and audiotape.

Collecting and Classifying ◄

Beyond naturalistic observation are two important science activities, *collecting* and *classifying*. Although collecting specimens is somewhat different from naturalistic observation, the two activities often go hand in hand, especially when it comes to the collection and classification of rock, mineral, plant, or animal specimens. Also, a person who has made several observations of anything has a collection of observations, even though nothing may have been collected.

Scientific classifiers use names, numbers, or other symbols to organize like and unlike materials. Finding names, or making up names, becomes an important problem in some fields of science, like chemistry or biology. Of course, the names do not come first: the first problem is to classify the things usefully.

Think about a collection of rock and mineral specimens numbering from several dozen to several hundred. There is no single, correct way to classify them, even though a scientific classification that may appear to be the "correct" one already exists. A collection may be classified in many different ways according to any one or more of the following characteristics or criteria:

▼ Size of specimen

▼ Color

▼ Crystalline form

▼ Chemical composition

- ▼ Hardness
- ▼ Density or specific gravity
- ▼ Fossil content
- ▼ Geological origin
- ▼ Geographical origin
- ▼ Money value
- ▼ Other criteria

The needs or purposes of the person doing the classifying usually determine the kind of classification used. This does not mean that there is something wrong with a standard scientific classification. Classifications usually help scientists satisfy certain specific needs:

- ▼ To help show relations between different subgroups (such as species or genus in biology)
- ▼ To help make communication about the things clear and accurate

There are good reasons for using scientific names for flowering plants, for example, because of the confusion caused by their common names. Also, since scientific classifications and names are widely published, many people find them useful for nonscientific purposes. You should know about them and use them where they will serve you best. Even so, you may find that you have very good reason for working out your own classification for your own special purposes. For example, you might classify insects in your locality several different ways:

▼ Those that attack garden plants and those that do not, or are beneficial

▼ Those that are "pests" to campers or picnickers and those that are not

▼ Those that attack other insects and perhaps help to control them

Is such a collection and classification a science investigation? Not necessarily. It may be only a reporting of facts or information that other people have already discovered.

A collection and/or classification may be acceptable as a science investigation when it is used to test a hypothesis or to prove something. Many important scientific discoveries or hypotheses have been largely based upon the collecting and classifying of specimens. Ideas about the evolution of species proposed by the nineteenth-century English naturalist Charles Darwin is an important example.

A collection may also be called a **survey.** In the next chapter we will explore the many ways in which surveys may be used as scientific methods.

CHAPTER 9

Surveys and Controlled Surveys

A survey is one of the most important and widely used methods of science, even though it is seldom discussed as part of a school science class. A simple survey would be to count the number of people living in an area such as a few blocks in a small town. Less simple would be a survey that tallied and analyzed the inhabitants by age, sex, size of household, occupation, and the like. The U.S. Census attempts to do this for the entire country every 10 years. One could take a count of the different kinds of trees, birds, or other animals in an area, and that, too, would be a survey. Most people would not think of these examples as science projects. However, if these censuses or enumerations are done completely and accurately they can be called scientific as well as naturalistic observation.

For a school science investigation you may make several kinds of surveys. Let's look into an investigation of students' reaction times as a useful and interesting example of survey science. Some of you may not be clear about the differences between this kind of survey and an experiment. In an experiment, you would be trying to change something to learn what happens as a result of the change. Not so in this investigation. Here you are measuring reaction times, not trying to change them.

Measuring Reaction Times ←

An easy method for measuring reaction time is the "ruler-drop" method. The only materials required are an ordinary 12-inch ruler with a 30-centimeter metric scale along one side, and, of course, the usual note-taking materials. Let's say Joe agrees to be your test subject. Seat Joe with his forearm resting on a table or desk, his hand extended over the edge, and his finger and thumb about 1 centimeter apart, ready to catch the ruler when you drop it. Hold the ruler with the zero

end of the metric scale down and place it between Joe's finger and thumb but not touching either. Try to not give Joe any advance signal that you are about to drop the ruler. When you drop it, he catches it between his forefinger and thumb. You then measure on the centimeter scale how much of the ruler (how many centimeters and millimeters) passed between Joe's finger and thumb before he caught it.

You can do this as a classroom survey by pairing off the students so that each one measures the reaction time of his or her partner. You raise interest in this survey by asking them, "Do boys or girls have faster reaction times? Or is there no important difference?" Those questions may also encourage the teacher to regard your project as real science and work with you.

Demonstrate to the students how to do the ruler-drop measure, then give the partners time to practice before they do the actual measuring for their records. Each subject should plan to make five good measurements of his or her partner. Have them write down the measurements on small slips of paper or 3" × 5" index cards. The sex of the person measured should be noted but not the name. Have each person doing the measuring draw a circle around the middle value of the five measurements on the slip. This is the *median* (which we will discuss in more detail later in the chapter on statistics).

Collect the slips and have everyone prepare to make two lists of the median reaction times, one for boys and one for girls. You then read off from each slip the sex and the median figure for the person and have everyone note them on their lists.

When all their lists are complete, the students then figure the **average, or mean,** for each sex. (These calculations may also be done outside of class time.) When they are finished and can agree on the means for boys and for girls, you are then ready for them to discuss the meaning of any difference between the means. You should point out that there is sure to be *some difference* between the means in a complex measurement such as this one. The big question is how much difference between the means does it take to be a meaningful difference, a *significant difference*? In our discussion of statistics in chapter 13 we will see how scientists and statisticians deal with this question.

Is this example of measuring reaction times of a group of people a case study or a survey? There is no clear distinction between them.

In this example your subjects are actively taking part in the investigation. Consequently, they may be seen as being more than just subjects under observation.

You can improve the validity of this investigation by having other students in other classrooms, preferably of the same age or grade level, make similar studies of their reaction times. In this expanded study you are almost sure to find that the average or mean reaction times of the two sexes differ among the groups. Now you can more accurately determine whether there is a real difference between the reaction times of boys and of girls.

Survey Variables ←

Like an experiment, a survey may include an independent and a dependent variable or other related variables. Consider an investigation based on this question: How much is the playing of musical instruments by children related to the playing of musical instruments by their parents? In conducting an experiment, we would have to rear children according to a prepared plan—some with parents who play musical instruments and some with parents who do not. After ten or twelve years we would compare the groups to see what we could learn.

No one, obviously, is going to do such an experiment. The only workable method is to take a survey of many parents and children. As in an experiment, the hypothesis would include a statement of two variables that the investigator suspects might be related: (1) the playing of musical instruments by parents and (2) the playing of musical instruments by their children. The hypothesis might be: "There is a statistically significant relation between the playing of musical instruments by children and the playing of musical instruments by the parents of these children."

As in an experiment, a survey may require that constants be maintained. For instance, in classifying children into two groups, those who play instruments and those who do not, we would not want to allow biases to creep into the findings. We would try to ensure, for example, that all of the children came from families of similar income level, similar educational level, and so forth. Or, to take a different approach, we would try to do a good job of randomizing the families so that all income levels, educational levels, and the like would be fairly represented in both groups of children.

Such a survey would require interviewing the children or their parents face to face, by telephone, by mail, or in some other manner, using a suitable questionnaire.

In the end, we would hope to have enough information on enough children and their parents to make a decision about the hypothesis. Would an affirmative answer ("Yes") to the hypothesis tell us that the parents' playing was a cause, or the main cause, of the children's playing? Probably not. The causes of such playing are complicated. There are many other variables that may be part of the answer. However, as a result of our survey, we may find that the two variables are related.

A Controlled Survey ◄───────────────

A survey can also be controlled in much the same way as in a controlled experiment. The people in the survey are called the "sample" of the larger population. For example, if you survey 30 students in a classroom, out of all of the people in the world they are your "sample." In a controlled survey, you need to divide the subjects surveyed into two groups, the survey sample and the control or survey control sample. For example, if you were to investigate the effects of the hours spent watching TV have on siblings (brothers or sisters), you would create two samples, one with siblings (the survey sample) and one without siblings (the control sample). In all other respects the two groups should be as alike as possible. Give each person in the two groups a questionnaire that includes the question, "How much time do you spend watching TV per day?" When you get the questionnaires back, you can analyze them to learn if there is a significant difference between the survey group and the control group.

Survey science differs in this important way from experimental science: In doing a survey, you try not to change anything. However, you may use the results of the survey to change things. You may then need to do another survey to learn what effects, if any, the changes had.

Your undertaking of a controlled survey can be honest and scientific. It can also be an excellent basis for a display in a science fair.

CHAPTER 10

Measurement

easurement is a most important part of the sciences. Not only do scientists use measuring instruments of many kinds, they also have been in the forefront of developing new measuring tools and standards.

SI Units

While some countries continue to use their own customary measuring units (in the United States we use pounds, feet, gallons, and so on), the International System of Units (SI Units, from the French *Système International*) has been adopted worldwide for both commercial and scientific purposes. The basic SI units include the following:

- ▼ **Meter:** length or distance
- ▼ **Kilogram:** mass, more commonly called "weight"
- ▼ **Second:** time
- ▼ **Ampere:** electric current
- ▼ **Candela:** light and other radiation
- ▼ **Mole:** comparing other substances to the molecular weight of a certain form of carbon
- ▼ **Kelvin:** temperature

From these basic units come many "derived units." An example is the measurement of area, for which the unit, called the square meter, is derived from the basic length unit or meter. Another example is the measurement of velocity, commonly called "speed," for which the unit, called meters per second, is measured from the basic meter traveled.

How to Measure ◄——————————————————

To measure something usually means taking a widely accepted tool, such as a meter stick, and comparing it with the thing to be measured. Practical measuring methods abound, ranging from astronomers' methods for estimating the Earth's distance in light-years from celestial objects to micrometers and other tools used for measuring very small objects. Scientists are even finding ways to measure the sizes of atomic particles, their "spin," and other characteristics.

For this discussion of measurement, the metric system will be used in all examples. If you have a meter stick at hand for reference it will be useful. If you do not have one, the commonly available foot ruler with a metric scale along one side (about 30 centimeters, each divided into tenths or millimeters) will do.

Let's say that you want to measure the width of a room with a meterstick. You agree to measure it to the nearest millimeter (or 0.001 meter). If you are not familiar with measuring in the metric system, note that a millimeter is equal to roughly $1/32$ inch.

If the room you are measuring has a hard floor, you can make a pencil mark at the end of the meter stick each time you lay it out across the room. Or, if there is a carpet, you can stick a pin in it to mark the end of the stick. Let's say that you find there are five whole meters and a part of a meter that looks like figure 10.1 at the arrow point. This would read 5.823 meters.

Multiple Measurements ◄——————————————

But one measurement is not enough if you intend to understand the problems of measurement. You should try to get an independent second measurement. To do this, have a friend make a measurement without telling him or her ahead of time what result you got.

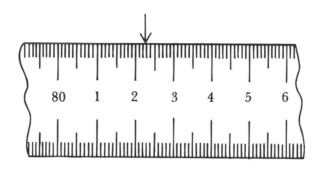

Figure 10.1

Arrow pointing to 0.823 meter mark.

Suppose your friend measures the room using the same tools and methods and gets a result of 5.834. You now have two measurements: 5.823 and 5.834 meters. Which is right? No one knows. What if you measure it again? Good, but would that prove to be the correct measurement any more than the first two? Not likely. No one can know the "true" measurement. We must face the problem that there is no perfect way to measure it. Two people will probably not measure anything, even the width of a room, exactly alike. Even the same person is not likely to get the same measurement twice, especially if one allows enough time between measurements to forget the first measurement.

Just as important, no two meter sticks or other measuring instruments are exactly alike, either. There is no such thing as a perfect measuring instrument, just as there is no perfect measurement.

To get as good a measurement as is reasonably possible of the width of the room, it is necessary to take several independent measurements. Let's say you end up with five different values: (1) 5.823, (2) 5.834, (3) 5.829, (4) 5.830, and (5) 5.825. Now we have a statistical question: Which one shall we choose to be the width of the room? If we take the arithmetical average, or mean, we get 5.828 meters. This average, we see, is not any one of the values we got by actual measurement. Is it the "correct" measurement? All we can say is that it is probably very close to it.

If you were measuring the diameter of a marble with a micrometer, you would find the same problems. Several independent measurements would probably give you several different values. Again, no one would know which was the correct diameter. Once again, there would be a statistical problem in choosing a number to represent the diameter, the "true" diameter, which no one can know.

Scientists have understood this uncertainty about measuring for a long time. It seems to surprise others, however. Some people react to this discovery by saying, "Well, if I can't really know what the measurement is, why bother trying to make it exact?" The reason is that scientists and others who keep working out better ways to measure things are trying to communicate better. Reporting scientific findings to others is an important part of scientific method, as you know, and communication among scientists has been helped immeasurably by better and better systems of measurement.

Dealing with Uncertainty in Measurement ◄

How do we deal with this uncertainty, besides pretending it does not exist? In the most ordinary measuring of things, one reasonably careful measurement is all that is needed. Most people will settle for that, believing that they know the length of a thing, or its time, or its weight, and so forth. However, many scientific and technical workers must work as nearly as they can to the limits of the accuracy of their instruments and methods. They must also report to others what those limits of accuracy are. That is why there is need for ways to express these limits.

Here is one method: Let's say that you are measuring across a piece of paper with a scale such as a ruler divided into centimeters (cm) and tenths of a centimeter (or millimeter). You want to express your measurement as centimeters to the nearest tenth, such as 23.7 cm. (See figure 10.2.)

As you measure, you will see that the edge of the paper is not quite on one of the marks showing tenths, so pick the tenth mark that the edge is nearest to. That is, pick 23.7, not 23.6. (See figure 10.3.)

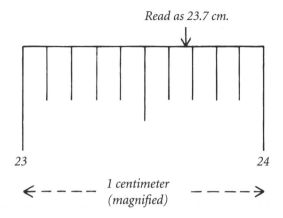

Read as 23.7 cm.

23   24

1 centimeter
(magnified)

Figure 10.2

However, you do not want anyone to think that you are claiming that the paper measured exactly 23.7 cm. Instead, you would like to tell others that you are reading the scale to within one-half of a division either way from a scale mark. (See figure 10.4.)

One-half of one-tenth is 0.05 in decimal notation. This is why you put "+ 0.05 cm" after your measurement figure. For example: 23.7 + 0.05 cm (which reads, "23.7 plus or minus five-hundredths of a centimeter").

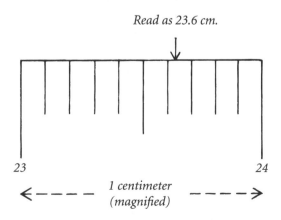

Read as 23.6 cm.

23   24

1 centimeter
(magnified)

Figure 10.3

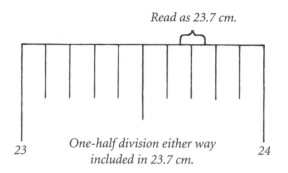

Read as 23.7 cm.

23

*One-half division either way
included in 23.7 cm.*

24

Figure 10.4

For another method of expressing uncertainty, let's go back to the measurement of the width of a room. There we made five measurements and reported the mean as 5.828 meters. If we had wanted to express the same measurement in millimeters (mm) instead of in meters, we could have reported 5,828 mm. Remember, 5,828 mm is the average of five measurements of which the shortest was 5,823 mm and the longest was 5,834 mm. This spread from lowest to highest we call the "range" of the 5 measures. We express the range as 11 mm by subtracting the shortest measurement from the longest.

Our mean of 5,828 mm is 6 mm below the top of the range and 5 mm above the bottom. We may also want people to know the range when we report the mean of several measurements. This is recorded as: 5,828 ± 6 mm. Or, we could report it in its meter unit: 5.828 ± 0.006 m.

This system, using the mean to express the range, is an overly simplified explanation of the method, but it does show how the system works.

There is yet another way to express the uncertainty of measurements. As a simple example, let's say that you are measuring a rod with a meter stick and find that it is just under 1 meter. That is reported as 0.999 m (or 999 mm) because you wish to report that the measurement is nearer to 0.999 m than to 1.000 m (or nearer to 999 mm than to 1,000 mm). You are saying that the range is within 1 mm out of about 1,000 mm. Therefore, you report your measurement as 0.999 m with an "error" of 1 part per 1,000. The term "error" is not used in this method to mean that you made a mistake; it is another way of expressing the usual inaccuracy of any measurement.

Suppose, however, that you take the same meter stick and measure a room that is close to 10 m (or 10,000 mm) across. You find that several measurements range from 9,995 to 10,005, or a net range of 10 mm. This, too, shows an error of about 10 parts in 10,000 or 1 part in 1,000, as in the previous example.

To say that these measurements are accurate to 1 part in 1,000, we must assume that your meter stick is "exactly" 1 meter long. Of course, we cannot claim that because we are working on the assumption that no two things are exactly alike (including your meter stick and some master meter stick).

All measuring instruments, including wooden meter sticks, do change from their original dimensions. This unstable nature of things is part of our measurement problem. The changes that come with variations in temperature, humidity, and other factors must always be expected as part of our measuring and should be allowed for in our reporting if we are trying for high accuracy. Scientists working on one of the most important measuring problems, the measurement of the speed of light, using the best equipment and methods they can devise, must still allow for the uncertainty of their measurements. Thus, they report the velocity of light in a vacuum as 299,792,456 ± 1.1 meters per second.

We have discussed three different ways of reporting the uncertainty of measurements: (1) Reference to one-half of the smallest scale division; (2) Reference to a range of several values above and below the mean of those values; (3) The error in parts per 1,000, parts per million, or the like. Now that you better understand how the "pros" work with uncertainty in measurement, you may be able to handle it fairly easily while you do your own science investigations.

CHAPTER 11

Record Keeping

Records are the foundation of a report. If you were to work in secret with no thought of ever reporting to others, your record keeping would be altogether your own concern. However, if you want others to recognize what you have done, your records must always be designed to help you in reporting to others. The records themselves should bear inspection by anyone. They should tell anyone reasonably familiar with the kind of work you did all he or she would need to know about your investigation.

Do not depend upon remembering things. Keep a diary or diary-like notes. Each time you do something, write it down or dictate it into a tape recorder for later transcription, record it in a chart or table, make a sketch or a diagram of it, or take a photograph of it. And always, always, date your record, including clock time if this may be important because your diary is also a chronology. For most of your recording use a bound notebook (not loose-leaf), one that lies flat when opened. Write with pen—not pencil. Do not expect to erase. If you need to change a statement, draw a single line through it but leave it so that it can be read, then rewrite the statement. It is best to write double-space in the notebook.

It is perfectly good procedure to write ideas for other investigations in the diary record book as you go along as well as write thoughts about what you might have done better—or thoughts about how well you did do! Think of your record keeping as a rich source of material for your report. It will contain a great amount of material that you will not put into your final report, but the material should be there if needed. Be generous in your record keeping.

If, in your absence, it should be necessary for another person to make observations for you, make certain that he or she is well trained in the work and will do the record keeping at least as well as you would yourself. Identify your substitute's part of the work in the record.

If you find it necessary to make records separate from your notes—such as tape recordings, diagrams, photographs, and charts—number and date each one; refer to them in your notes so that they are tied in to the chronological record.

All of these original records must be preserved. Do not copy and then throw out the originals. Keep them. It is so easy to make mistakes in copying. Then, too, there is a temptation to edit in the copying—to change something so that it looks better. If you need a copy, make one, of course, but KEEP THE ORIGINALS!

All of these record-keeping requirements! Why? Remember that you will forget. Important details may become vague after a while. Or someone may ask a question about your work that you might not have thought about. Your records can help you in your answer. And (who knows?) a hundred years from now someone may be saying. "See! Here is the original record of an early investigation, done long before the fame of later years. Isn't it nice that we have this?"

In the following list other important methods for making records are described. Some are costly, and if your budget does not cover them, that is okay. Just try to make sure that your note-taking and other data-collection methods are done as fully and as accurately as you can make them.

Pictorial and Audio Records

- ▼ Try to have a camera ready to photograph key aspects of your investigations.
- ▼ Make sketches, even though you may not be a "great artist." Your sketches can be an important part of your record.
- ▼ Diagram the layout of your apparatus.

▼ Use a video camera if you have one when you need to get a combination of sound and action with the subjects you observe.

▼ Use audio recording if there are sounds involved in your investigation. If you interview people for your project, always try to get a sound recording on a tapc recorder. Of course, get permission to record in advance from the people you interview.

Charts and Graphs ◄────────────

Charts and graphs are especially useful for displaying large amounts of data in your report or display, and for putting the data in forms that people can easily grasp. As you learn how to create good charts and graphs, these skills will almost surely be of benefit to you in your schooling as you try to master material produced by others. You can work from some of the examples in this book, or read up on the making of charts and graphs in the references in the Bibliography.

CHAPTER 12

Causality and Theory

One of the most important goals of doing science is to try to learn more about why things are the way they are, or happen as they appear to happen. As we better understand the causes of things, or "causality," we can better manage them. We can develop theories about why things happen and come to some conclusions about why things work as they do. This knowledge can lead to practical solutions to particular problems.

First, we should look at the term "theory." In ordinary usage, the theory usually means something like "unproven," or maybe even, "not true." But professional scientists use the term to refer to an explanation for something that happens, or its **causal explanation.** As part of any science project or investigaton, you should try to prepare a theory or explanation as to why something happens as it does, or why it does not happen as expected.

For example, let's say you do a survey of people's reaction times as discussed in chapter 9. You might find that boys react somewhat faster than girls of the same ages, or you might find that girls react faster than boys. Or you might make a survey of your classmates and find that girls carry around more pocket money than do boys. Then what? Right away, some people will ask, "Why is that?" They want a "causal explanation." They want to know why things happen in a certain way and not in other ways. Finding good, solid, causal explanations, or theories, is a primary goal of most scientists.

Causal Multiplicity and Causal Chains

If you were to do a pocket-money survey and found that girls carry more pocket money than boys of the same age, you probably could find many possible explanations. The girls may earn more or spend less, on average, than do boys of the same age. Or maybe the finding was just a fluke. In one such survey of a classroom of students, the total pocket money for the girls was far above that of the boys because one girl happened to have a large amount of money with her that she had received as a gift, which she was planning to deposit in her bank after school. The problem of things having many possible causes is called causal multiplicity.

The tendency in our society is to be coached in identifying single, **primary causes** of most events in our lives. In effect, we become trained not to look for the many, many causes of those events. But a major principle of causality is that there *are* many causes for anything that happens. All things and events are actually the result of **causal chains,** a series of causes and effects.

A very simple example of a causal explanation is that when you press the key for the "X" on a computer, you will get an "X" on your screen. Or if you make the proper movements with fingers and pencil, an "X" will appear on your paper. In both of these cases, there is a simple causal explanation. But if you look further, you can see a chain of causes in which each cause is an effect of a cause that went before it. To get the "X" on the screen or on paper, you had to find the "X" on the keyboard, and to do that, you had to know what the letter "X" looks like, and so on.

Your Hypothetical Cause

As you do a science investigation, you usually are putting together a cause-effect relation of some kind. You work at making clear that one major cause, a primary cause, produced the effect that you want and that you express in your hypothesis: The bean plants in Planter A grew better than those in Planter B because of the hypothetical cause—

baking soda in the irrigation water for Planter A. When you express your hypothesis you are making less important the many other causes for the growth in Planter A because, in a sense, by comparason those many other causes are *not* as important as the **hypothetical cause.** That's okay! That is the way to do good science for a science fair. (Note that hypothetical cause does not mean a cause that may be wholly imaginary in this sense. Instead it means the cause as put forth in your hypothesis.)

First Causes ◄─────────────────────────

Consider causal chains again. Where does a causal chain start? This is a tough question. Anytime someone suggests a "first cause," someone else is almost sure to ask, "How do you explain that? What caused that?" You may not be able to find a "first cause" for your project, but you may be able to develop a series of investigations showing how causes and effects connect with other causes and effects.

CHAPTER 13

Evaluating Results: Statistics, Probability, and Proof

When you do an experiment or a survey comparing two sets of people or things, the job of statistics is to show whether you have a *significant difference* between the two sets. A small difference between the averages or means may or may not be significant. How do you decide?

The experts use a system that has two basic stages:

1. They examine the data to find out how much variation there already is among the specimens.

2. They use that variation as a basis for deciding that the **experimental difference,** or **survey difference,** is enough to be a significant difference.

Another useful statistic is the *median*. In the test of reaction times by the ruler-drop method, we asked each partner to measure five catches by the other partner, then took the average, or mean. We might instead have chosen the number in the middle, which is called the median. It can often be as useful as the mean and takes less time to calculate.

Statistically Meaningful Results ◄

The example of taking five measurements across a room in the measurement chapter may be thought of as a simple method among all the possible measurements that could be made. We could also set up a program of making many such measurements, or of many people each making many measurements, so that one might eventually have thousands or millions of measurements.

The large, unknown number of measurements of which any one measurement is considered a sample can be known only from the sample. This is like eating cookies from a cookie jar. No matter how enjoyable the first, second, or third, we will never know how good the remaining cookies are from the samples only. We can only predict or infer that the uneaten cookies, the population from which the sample came, are like the sample.

How do scientists judge whether their sample of measurements (or findings expressed other ways) fairly represents all possible measurements? Let's say that Alice is doing an experiment as her science project in which she has planted popcorn seeds in two planters to test the value of a fertilizer. She is going to compare the two plantings, one with the fertilizer and the other without but otherwise grown under uniform conditions. To keep the numbers small for quick, easy measuring, let's say that each planter has five healthy, growing plants. Suppose that Alice measures the heights of the five plants in one of the planters and finds the following:

Plant A	57.2 cm
Plant B	57.2 cm
Plant C	57.2 cm
Plant D	57.2 cm
Plant E	57.2 cm

What? All the same? Most of us who have had experience with growing things would immediately say that this is highly improbable, that it is just a coincidence that all the plants would be precisely the same height. Correct! It is a matter of chance or probability. Probability, you will find, is the main theme in the evaluation of scientific findings. Suppose, now, that Alice's measuring had brought the following results:

Plant A	57.9 cm
Plant B	55.7 cm
Plant C	58.4 cm
Plant D	59.2 cm
Plant E	57.3 cm

"That's more like it," we would say. We expect differences in things, especially in living, growing things. That is, it is highly probable that the heights would not be all the same.

Now, whether we like the sample or not, it is *all* we know about the larger population of plants that Alice's supply of seed might grow. Suppose, again, that Ken planted 100 seeds from the same supply as Alice's and under very much the same conditions. Then suppose he went to work measuring them at the same stage as Alice's plants. We would like to see how the sizes vary in this much larger sample, so we make a *frequency distribution* (see figure 13.1) showing the sizes. That

Figure 13.1

Frequency Distribution of 100 Corn Plants

Number of corn plants at each height	50	51	52	53	54	55	56	57	58	59	60	61	62	63	64	65
14																
13																
12								x								
11						x		x	x							
10						x	x	x	x							
9					x	x	x	x	x	x						
8					x	x	x	x	x	x	x					
7				x	x	x	x	x	x	x	x					
6			x	x	x	x	x	x	x	x	x	x				
5			x	x	x	x	x	x	x	x	x	x				
4			x	x	x	x	x	x	x	x	x	x	x			
3		x	x	x	x	x	x	x	x	x	x	x	x			
2		x	x	x	x	x	x	x	x	x	x	x	x	x		
1	x	x	x	x	x	x	x	x	x	x	x	x	x	x		x

(1 plant 50 cm high; 3 plants 51 cm high)

Height, centimeters. (Rounded to nearest centimeter)

is, an "X" mark is made for each corn plant over its height measurement, which is listed along the bottom of the chart.

We see that there are not many of the shortest and tallest plants but more of each size in the middle of the range. If we drew a line over the tops of the columns of sizes (and if we had many more specimens measured and recorded) the lines, or line graphs, would look something like the one in figure 13.2.

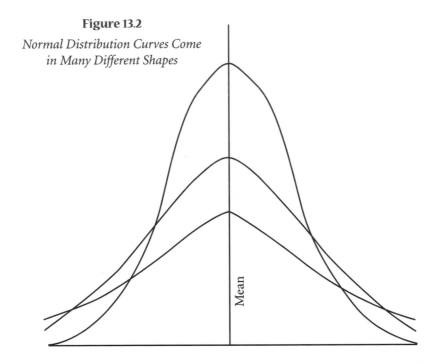

Figure 13.2

Normal Distribution Curves Come in Many Different Shapes

Mean

Such a distribution of a large number of things (and it must be large, preferably in the thousands) is called a **normal distribution.** Many things show normal distribution when they are measured and graphed like this, for example, the heights of large numbers of people picked at random and the amounts of food eaten per person per year. This widespread nature of things to show normal distribution has been used by scientists and statisticians to work out ever more meaningful designs for science investigations. Most modern scientists are thinking about the statistics they will use to analyze their findings from the beginning or planning stages of their investigations. They are saying something like this: "I don't want my experiment to come out as some queer, quirky thing that proves nothing. How must I plan now so that in the end my results will be statistically meaningful?" Scientists know, however, that there can be no perfect answer to their questions. They can always, just by chance, get results that show unexpected quirks.

Nevertheless, as a scientist does her investigation, she is trying to uncover some meaningful results. This means more than just saying, "Yes" or "No" to the hypothesis. It means going beyond the small number of subjects she may be dealing with in her experiment or survey. It means having confidence that her findings may be stretched, or generalized, to any larger group of similar subjects. Did ingredient Q seem to prevent sunburn in the experimental group of people who used it? If so, and if that experimental group fairly represents the larger population, we may then reasonably expect that ingredient Q will prevent sunburn in most of the larger population.

The use of random choices in the first stages of an investigation means more than just helping to keep the scientist's prejudices from affecting the results. It helps to assure that the sample of people, or other subjects, used in the investigation will allow us to generalize to the larger group that the sample is intended to represent.

Can You Prove It?

Let's say that Alice is doing an experiment as her science project in which she has planted popcorn seeds in two planters to test the value of a fertilizer. She uses the controlled experiment design.

To the experimental group she adds a chemical fertilizer, urea, a nitrogen compound that may be put into the soil or dissolved in the water given the plants. Her independent variable is the addition of the urea to the experimental group. Her dependent variable, if she observes one, is the difference in growth rate (height or weight) of the plants in her two planters.

At a proper time in her experiment, she measures the heights of the plants with the following results:

TABLE 13.1 HEIGHTS OF CORN PLANTS IN ALICE'S EXPERIMENT

	Control Group (no urea)	Experimental Group (Urea: 2 grams per liter of water)
	57.9 cm	60.3 cm
	55.7	60.0
	58.4	57.6
	59.2	61.2
	57.3	58.9
Totals	288.5 cm	298.0 cm
Means	57.7 cm	59.6 cm

Difference between means: 59.6 − 57.7 = 1.9 cm

We see that there is a difference between the means (commonly called average) of the two groups. The difference is 1.9 cm in favor of the experimental group; the average height of the plants in that group is 1.9 cm taller than the height of the plants in the control group. This looks good.

"See!" Alice says. "Adding urea to the experimental planting has made the corn grow faster." Can she be sure of this? No, she cannot. Maybe it was a chance happening that she got five taller growing plants in the experimental group and five shorter growing plants in the control. She should not make any decision just yet. She should get someone to make a good statistical treatment (unless she can do it herself) that would go beyond comparing the mean heights of the two groups.

A statistical analysis would show how much the heights vary among themselves. Then it would show how the means compare with a larger "population" of plants like Ken's 100 plants. Where would this larger population be found? It would be imagined, inferred, or hypothetical: it would be created out of the variability, the range, the scatter of her sample and the size of the sample. It would be created by the use of equations in statistics books.

Furthermore, a judgment would be made about the chance, or the probability, that the difference Alice found was or was not simply a chance difference. This, too, would be done by reference to appropriate tables in statistics books. Actually, the number of plants in Alice's experiment is too small (only five) to make it worth all of that analysis, yet her results are supported by agricultural research by professional scientists and by the experiences of the thousands of farmers who have found it useful to apply urea and other nitrogen compounds to their corn plantings.

With all of that support, why wouldn't scientists declare that they have *proven* the value of this treatment of corn? The problem lies partly in this question: How can you know when you have proven a thing to be true? And it lies partly in the way the words "prove" and "true" are used in mathematics and logic as compared to the way they are used in ordinary speech.

First, the mathematics and logic. You and I can agree that this is a true statement in arithmetic: $148 + 293 + 167 = 608$. That is, we follow certain rules of mathematics to prove whether the statement is an equality. Mathematicians would not agree, however, that we had proven it by following the rules of addition. They are more concerned about the sources of those rules. In the end, they would show that the statement was proven by agreeing on certain things about arithmetic and its rules.

In logic of the formal sort, proof would be much the same, as in this example:

If all wangtups have gitly speekrongs,

And if Q is a wangtup,

Then Q has gitly speekrongs.

Even though the statements do not mean anything in real life, if we accept the first and second statements as true, then the conclusion, the third statement, is also true. The "proof" is all right there in the statement. It has nothing to do with real people or things and their mixed-up ways.

Still, these simple examples do not do justice to mathematics and logic. Both are fascinating and powerful tools of thought or reasoning that humankind has created. The proof or truth of these examples, however, is so very much different from the kinds of proof that scientists are seeking that it becomes awkward to try to use the same language to describe them all. Even though mathematicians and logicians got there first with the terms "prove" and "true," scientists in recent times have pulled away from using these terms.

In ordinary experience as well there is a problem with these key words. Most people would say, "See, Alice *proved* it! It is *true* that urea makes corn grow faster." Or they might say, "That proves it! Hocus is better for a headache than Pocus," even though they may have used the medication only one time and their test has serious weaknesses. Or, again: "That proves it! Dreams do foretell the future. I knew that you were coming because I dreamed about it!"

These difficulties with the language, however, do not provide the main objection to the use of "prove" in scientific work. When we talk about "proving" something in science we are, in effect, predicting the future as well as examining the present. How much can we depend on something happening in the future just because today's scientific findings show it to be probable now?

In Alice's experiment, for example, she used only five plants in each planter. Such a small sample cannot tell us much about the larger population of future corn plantings, no matter how much statistical analysis we apply to it. However, let's do some more analysis of Alice's results to see how this helps us to learn about the predictive value of her findings. Let's rearrange the measurements of the corn plants according to height (see table 13.2).

Does this tell us more than a simple comparison of the means? Suppose her results in the experimental group had been as in table 13.3 (also ranked by height).

Here we see that the difference between the means of the two groups is the same as in table 13.2. But notice the range of heights in table 13.3. The experimental plants are not as uniformly taller than the control plants as they were in table 13.2. There is more variability. These results would provide a less reliable basis for predicting about future plantings.

TABLE 13.2 ALICE'S EXPERIMENT: TWO GROUPS COMPARED BY RANKING		
Control Group (ranked shortest to tallest)	Experimental Group (ranked shortest to tallest)	Difference
55.7 cm	57.6 cm	+1.9 cm
57.3	58.9	1.6
57.9	60.0	2.1
58.4	60.3	1.9
59.2	61.2	2.0
Totals 288.5 cm	298.0 cm	9.5 cm
Means 57.7 cm	59.8 cm Mean Difference +2.1	

I hope that you begin to agree, if you had not already known, that statistical treatment of data can reveal useful information. Finding the means and their difference is statistical analysis. Ranking the heights and comparing the pairs of plants is statistical analysis. These two ways of analyzing data are very elementary (even antiquated) when compared with the methods used by people with more mathematical and statistical knowledge.

Replicating and Expanding on Experiments ◄

How could Alice "prove" more, besides just making statistical analyses of her data? She could replicate the experiment. This would raise the predictive power of her test if results were as good as the first test or better, even though it would still not finally prove anything. We must accept this because there is always uncertainty about the future. Some things are more highly probable than others, of course. We are all fairly

	Control Group	Experimental Group	Difference
TABLE 13.3 ALICE'S EXPERIMENT: GREATER VARIABILITY			
	55.7 cm	57.6 cm	1.9 cm
	57.3	58.9	1.6
	57.9	60.0	+2.1
	58.4	60.3	+1.9
	59.2	61.2	+2.0
Totals	288.5 cm	298.0 cm	+9.5 cm
Means	57.7 cm	59.8 cm	Mean Difference +2.1

sure that the sun will come up tomorrow, while we may not be so sure that another planting of corn, treated as Alice's was treated, will turn out the same. So we are always dealing in probabilities.

Scientists like to show that their findings allow them to predict, or generalize, in another way than in the simple replication of an experiment or other investigation. Alice could expand her research in several ways:

Plan A: One experimental level of urea, applied in water (Alice's first plan).

Planter	Description
1	Control: no urea
2	Experimental: 2 g (grams) per liter of water used to water the plantings

Plan B: Three experimental levels of urea, applied in water

Planter	Description
1	Control; no urea
2	Experimental: 2 g urea per liter of water

3   Experimental: 4 g urea per liter of water

4   Experimental: 6 g urea per liter of water

Plan C: Three experimental levels of urea, applied in soil

Planter   *Description*

1   Control; no urea

2   Experimental: 10 g urea mixed in the soil

3   Experimental: 20 g urea mixed in the soil

4   Experimental: 30 g urea mixed in the soil

If she were to test both variables—two ways of applying urea and three different levels of urea—at the same time Alice would need an arrangement of planters (or outdoor plots) as in figure 13.3.

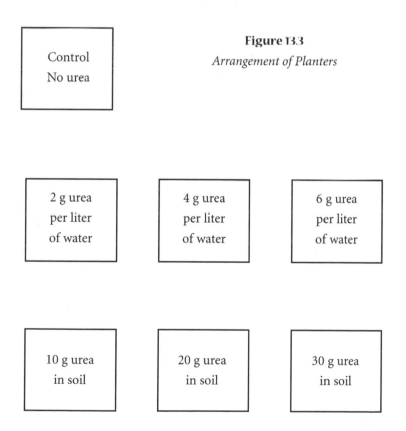

Figure 13.3

Arrangement of Planters

You may be interested in figuring out how many different experiments would be needed to test each of these plans one at a time against a control and against each different level of urea. Also consider that there are other nitrogen compounds that should be compared with urea; each should be applied in different amounts. Then there are other kinds of soil, other varieties of corn, other planting methods, other methods of applying the fertilizer, and other chemicals that may be as important as nitrogen for promoting healthy growth in the corn. Many of these variables would best be tested in combination with certain other variables. Therefore, the designs in some cases would be more complicated than in the above Plan C. For the most significant results, most of the experiments would be conducted all the way through to the mature stage of the crop. Therefore, the testing would need to be done outdoors in plots of land large enough to accommodate farm equipment.

Surely under these expanded conditions there would be enough "population" to make the results prove something! Well, perhaps not *surely,* but more so. And yet these methods would create other problems. Rarely would individual plants be measured in order to determine results. Instead, more gross measures, such as weighing the grain from each plot or weighing the grain and other plant matter, would be used. This would increase our confidence in the results in that they would not be affected so much by variations among individual plants as in Alice's small groups. Nevertheless, the different plots might vary as to quality of soil, drainage conditions, and the like, and so scientists have found that each "treatment" must be used over several smaller plots that are spread in a randomized pattern around an entire field. For example, instead of two larger plots, one experimental and one control, the experimental plot is divided into five smaller experimental plots (each given the same treatment) and the control plot is divided into five smaller control plots. These plots are distributed randomly throughout the entire field. As a consequence, we find that we are dealing with a small number of things (five plots) as in Alice's experiment with five corn plants. While this gives important improvements to the overall plan, it still shows somewhat the same problem of a small sample (small number of plots). As a consequence, the statistical treatment for such a study must be highly developed if you are to squeeze the most meaning out of the results.

All said and done, there is still uncertainty about the evaluation or results as there is elsewhere in scientific method. We must not be disheartened about this uncertainty, however. Unfortunately, many people have been oversold on science and its powers for finding out the "truth" about things. Others have shown disappointment over the way science has not been able to solve more problems. It is important to understand that scientific methods are the best that have been found so far for learning about many things, and that they are superior to ordinary, everyday, "commonsense" methods. That's why scientific methods are called "scientific"—they are better than unscientific methods. Yet, by comparison, humankind has been working with scientific methods only a short time. Not all kinds of human problems can be solved by using scientific kinds of knowledge, but those problems that might be solved by scientific methods seem to be limitless. Nevertheless, in spite of the uncertainty of science and the limited speed with which scientists can move into new areas, we must use scientific methods to find out all we can about the world and the people and things in it. Even with its uncertainty, it is still the best we have for trying to resolve many of the problems of humankind.

CHAPTER 14

How to Get Help in Evaluating Results

How serious should you be about evaluating the results of an investigation? Is it possible not to evaluate? Not to judge? As soon as you read the findings of a study, you probably start making a judgment about it. As long as you are going to evaluate the results you ought to make as good an evaluation as you can. Perhaps you do not know how to do statistical treatment beyond the simple comparison of the means of two groups, or the ranking of the measurements of specimens (as in Alice's experiment). Or, perhaps all you can do on your own is put the data in tables so that relations between variables can be easily seen and informally compared. After doing these things, if you still need more help, get it. There are people who may help, as well as books and computer software. First try the people near at hand.

If someone helps you do a "professional" statistical analysis of a simple set of data as in Alice's experiment, it may take an hour or more of time, depending upon how fluent the person is with statistics, whether your work must all be done with pencil and paper, or whether there is a computer available with the right software. If you have not taken high school algebra, you will have to depend upon others for processing your data.

Many teachers have had little practical need to learn statistical data processing, or they might not have the time necessary to help you. Others may not have taken statistics as part of their college program.

Consider asking another student who is more advanced in mathematics than you are. You might find a high school mathematics student who would like do a little digging in statistics in order to try his or her mathematical skills on a real problem. Perhaps a mathematics instructor might put you in touch with a math student who would help.

When you get help from someone in your school or community always remember to keep good notes about the people who help you and how they help. Then when you write up your report, or make your display, be sure to include a note about their assistance. That, and the benefit of possibly learning something new about science, is the only "pay" you may offer them.

On your own, you should learn as much about statistics as you can. You should get whatever computer software or books you can find in the school or community libraries on the design of experiments, surveys, statistics, and so forth. Even if on the whole a book is beyond your grasp, some reading of the introductory material may prove profitable. It may help you begin to grasp the language of statistics and to see how varied the patterns are. You should know that as different scientific methods are created, it becomes necessary to invent statistics to go with them.

In the field of statistics, as in most other human affairs, there is disagreement among the professionals about which statistics are best for a particular research design. Some prefer the kinds of statistics based upon "normal distribution" and consider them perfectly proper for many or even most analyses. Others disagree. They argue that there is the following weakness, especially for small samples, in the normal distribution kind of statistics:

1. You use the sample to imagine (or to infer or postulate) a "population" from which the sample was supposed to have been taken.

2. Then you compare the population with the sample in the statistical analysis to judge whether the sample was really representative or just a quirk.

The critics of normal distribution statistics say that this is circular reasoning, or reasoning in a circle, which is not good logic. That is, using *A* (the sample) to set up *B* (the population), then using *B* to judge *A* is poor reasoning or logic. Such critics of normal distribution statistics prefer to use "non-normal" or "nonparametric" methods.

As a beginner, you cannot be too concerned about such arguments and controversies among professionals, but even a hint will help you to see that mathematics (including statistics) is not standing still. New mathematics is constantly being created to fit the needs of people as their needs change.

Get Help in the Planning Stage

In your effort to seek help with your statistical treatment, you should try to get your consultant to be in on the planning stages of your project. Design of the investigation and statistical treatment should go together. It is altogether too easy to make an elaborate investigation only to reveal nothing significant. Remember the project for testing running speed as related to loss of sleep? Suppose that the experimenter had never heard of the counterbalancing plan and therefore did not use it. No matter how striking a difference between the running records of the two groups, the results would show nothing believable without the counterbalanced trials.

Of course, if you are to do as simple a project as measuring the boiling temperature of water, you will not need much statistical treatment of the data. However, if you make several different measurements at different times and try to do them independently (so that each new test is not influenced by your previous measurements), you may find considerable variation. You then may have something of a problem evaluating your results. You will want to consider questions like these: How much of the variation can be traced to differences in the water? In the apparatus? In other surrounding factors like atmospheric pressure? Your effort to find relations like these will probably lead to statistical treatment of the data.

For example, if you intend to find a relationship between the boiling (or freezing) temperatures of water when varying amounts of a salt are dissolved in the water, you will almost certainly want to graph the results and perhaps get some statistical counseling.

If you do a survey of the simple counting or census type, you will need less challenging statistical treatment than you would if you try to find a relationship between two variables, such as eating a good breakfast and performance on school tests.

How about evaluating the results of naturalistic observation? In the observing of people and things in their natural setting, you may accumulate large amounts of data that probably would adapt better to tables, graphs, and word descriptions than it would to statistical treatment. Your evaluation would come from comparing the results of your naturalistic observation with the results reported by other skillful observers.

The actual doing of scientific research is the work of most scientists. However, there are some scientists and others whose main concern is trying to show what can and cannot be reasonably demonstrated by scientific methods. These are two very different activities: (1) the active research, and (2) the reasoning, the analyzing, about what it means to do science and to do it "right." The people who do the second activity are primarily philosophers of science. They also may be scientists, of course, but they are working in an importantly different capacity when they are concerned with the reasoning, the logic, behind scientific discovery and explanation.

As the philosophers of science have explored deeper into what can and what cannot be proven in the work of scientists, they have come to agree substantially on this view: If you have a hypothesis that is expressed as a positive statement and that can be tested by scientific means, you are limited in what you can prove about it. You are limited in the sense that you cannot prove it to be permanently true, everywhere and always, but that you *can* prove it to be false. Take as an example the hypothesis that mice will grow normally on dried peas as their only food. You test the hypothesis on a group. The mice all grow normally. Have you permanently proven the hypothesis? Not necessarily. You could also encounter a group, or individual mice, that did *not* grow normally on that ration. In effect, it is possible to find evidence that will falsify any hypothesis, even though it may be generally valid, under special circumstances.

Professional scientists have learned to live reasonably comfortably with this kind of logic or reasoning. They have learned to live with the uncertainty that seems to be built into human knowledge—to live with the uncertainty while doing our best to reduce that uncertainty to something manageable.

So plan your project. Do what you can to get help from a statistician in judging the outcome of your research. Try to have that help in your planning stage. If you can't, do your project anyway. Get the results even if you may not be able to analyze them as fully as a professional would do. Maybe, someday, you will be able to come back to your report, analyze the results further, and say: "Well, see what I discovered, I think!"

CHAPTER 15

Publishing or Reporting

Why should you publish a report of your investigation? Because publishing helps to make good science better! Publishing a report of your investigation is an important part of doing science because it allows others to check up on your work and makes it possible for them to replicate it. It also makes your work known to others who may have been looking for answers to the same questions, or who may use your results as a jumping off point for their own investigations.

What Goes in Your Report?

To present your evidence, you must be able to make a report that is good in detail, that permits those who read it to find in it enough information that they may judge the validity of your findings, and, if they wish, to replicate your investigation. The following recommendations are general. You must make your report fit your investigation as best you can:

1. Introduction

State the question or problem you have tried to answer or the theory you wish to test. Your title may also state the question or problem, but expand it here in your introduction.

You may wish to put an "abstract" at the beginning of your report. This is for the benefits of readers who are not sure that they want to read your whole report. It tells the story in perhaps 100 to 200 words.

In your introduction you may want to tell what brought you to make this investigation—that is, what other explorations led up to it (not, of course, that you want to get a good grade or to win a prize!).

State your hypothesis. This narrows down your goal. Begin from a general theory, question, or problem, then try to be as specific as you can be in stating what you are trying to test.

You should plan to restate the hypothesis in your report, as necessary.

2. Procedure

Here you describe your methods and materials. You must always think of your readers as not being present to see the things you used and how you proceeded. What will they need to know about this? Could they take this description and replicate the study? (See chapter 11 for more on record-keeping.)

3. Results

In your notes, you will have recorded both method and results in a blend of records of various kinds. This is called raw data. However, in the writing of your final report, you will probably separate the two kinds of data into a methods section and a results section.

The methods section will be mainly word descriptions plus diagrams, photographs, and other methods used.

For the results section, if you recorded only small amounts of data, facts, and/or measurements, you may just include all of the raw data in your final report. If, on the other hand, you have mountains of raw data, it is unlikely that all of it should appear in your final report. Rather, it should be summarized in graphs and tables of various kinds, or by whatever means is best suited to your goal of presenting clear and convincing evidence.

The calculations of your statistical analysis need not be shown in full, but you must show the results of those calculations and identify the methods used. If you report a mean or average of 49.8, everybody knows what you mean. However, if you report a relationship between the two series of measurements, you must tell which statistical method you used to determine that relationship. With most statistical treatments you must explain your method.

How you judge the validity of your results will largely depend upon the extent to which you get into statistical analysis. Any statements you make will grow out of your understanding of the statistics, or will be made with help of your consultant in statistics.

In all of the above suggestions for making a report, there may be conflicts with other requirements. Your instructor in science may have different requirements for your report if you do a project under his or her guidance. You should comply with those standards unless, of course, you can convince your instructor of the desirability of doing things differently. Then, too, if you get as far as being published in a magazine or journal, your editor will have ideas about how to present your report. Even though you might not get published in a journal, you may find it interesting to go to a college or university library, find journals in your field of research, and see how the professionals are currently making their reports.

Much of this kind of reporting is dry, factual, and, in fact, not very interesting unless you are deeply into the subject. Yet, occasionally a science paper turns up that is written with style, wit, and grace. And at no conflict with the content! What a pleasure! If you have found that you can write in an interesting style, do try to apply your style to the writing of your science report.

How to Publish ◄─────────────────────────

In the end, how do you publish? Displaying your work in a science fair at your school is one way to publish. That way, however, is limited, may not reach many people, and therefore may not encourage others to replicate your investigation. A school or school district can help promote better publishing. A science teacher can develop a "science journal" for the school by copying the reports of science investigations. Such a journal need not be bound like a magazine. It can be loose-leaf. Or, the pages of an individual report can be stapled and two or more reports can be held together with large clips or with rubber bands. Copies of the school science journal can be supplied to each classroom in the school, even though most of them are not science rooms. Such publishing can help many others to understand better how science works and encourage them not to be afraid of science.

Seed Germination Test

By doing a seed germination test you can make sure that you have good, viable seeds that will sprout and grow. If you can, buy or borrow petri dishes, which are designed for culturing seeds and other organisms. If you don't have petri dishes, you can use two ordinary saucers that have smooth edges.

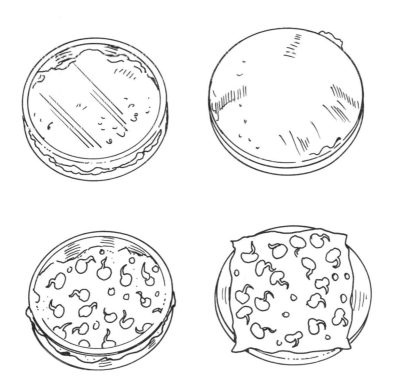

Use a piece of paper towel cut to a size that covers the bottom of the dish. Moisten the paper towel, then scatter around it a precise number of seeds, for example, 25 or 50. Take another piece of paper towel, cut it to size, moisten it, and use it to cover the seeds. If you are using saucers, turn one of them upside down and place it over the other one.

Keep the seeds at room temperature for a few days. You want the seeds to be kept moist but not covered by water, so moisten both the top and bottom papers periodically. Look at the seeds each day until all the seeds that are going to sprout have sprouted (not all seeds will germinate). Then count the seeds that have germinated and figure out the percentage of sprouted to unsprouted seeds.

Use that percentage to decide how many seeds to plant in your main experiment. For example: If you want to grow 50 plants in your main experiment and the germination test shows that 70 percent sprouted, then divide 50 by 0.70 (or 70 percent). That works out to be 71 seeds that you need to plant in each planter in order to get about 50 good plants in each.

Now for the main experiment. Remove the same amount of soil from each filled planter, enough to cover the seeds to a depth of about 1 centimeter. Scatter the seeds over the soil, then cover them with about 1 centimeter of the soil you removed. Carefully water the soil, trying to keep it evenly moist, especially during this period of seed germination. Use equal amounts of water for each planter.

Now, how do you decide which planter is "experimental" and which is "control"? The goal here is not to let your biases enter into your choice. An easy way to decide is to toss a coin: Heads, planter A is the experimental and planter B the control. Tails, planter B is the experimental and planter A the control.

Now you are ready to go ahead with your experiment, using whatever factor you are testing as the independent variable—a fertilizer element in the experimental planter, a difference in the lighting, in temperature, or whatever you decide you want to test.

During the seed germination test, of course, you should be keeping very detailed records of everything you do.

More Reaction-Time Methods

Here are two more methods of measuring a person's reaction times. A quick and easy way to compare the reaction times of a group of people is to have them stand in a row, one behind the other, facing the same direction.

Each person holds one hand at his or her back, ready to receive a touch signal from the person behind, and the other hand ready to touch the hand of the person in front. One person with a stopwatch gives a signal to the first person at the back of the row, who then starts the "reaction" along the row by touching the hand of the person in front, and so on to the end of the row. The timer watches for the last person's signal, and records the time for the group. This method does not give an individual measurement for each person, as does the ruler-drop method. It is, however, a quick and easy method for finding a mean reaction time for comparing groups by sex, height, weight, age, and so forth. You can call this method the hand-to-hand reaction time.

Another way to use the ruler-drop method is the eye-to-foot version. Seat the subject so that he or she holds one foot near a doorjamb without touching it, elevating it about knee height above the floor. Another person holds a meter stick against the doorjamb, with the zero end at the person's toe, ready to drop it. At the drop, the seated person tries to catch the meter stick by pressing his or her foot against the doorjamb.

GLOSSARY

anecdotal evidence   Evidence given out of one's experience, told as a story. As evidence, usually judged to be of lower quality than scientific evidence.

average   See MEAN.

bell curve   See NORMAL DISTRIBUTION.

bias   Leaning away from the expected normal, norm, or standard. Sometimes used as a synonym for prejudice.

blind experiment   In a blind experiment, the individual subject is not told whether he or she is in an experimental group or in a control group. See PLACEBO.

case study   The scientific observation of a single individual or event that is self-contained, although the term may be applied to a study that is part of a larger group or series of studies.

causal chain   Events that come in a series, or in certain sequences, in such a way that preceding events are said to "cause" events that come later.

cause, causality   Conditions *necessary* for a specific thing to happen. An event that *always* precedes or goes before another event. In science, the terms refer to a probable explanation or theory.

classification   The separation of things or people into groups because of their likenesses and differences.

coincidence   Two or more things happening together by chance, with no causal connection identified between them.

collection of detailed data   Information, facts, and figures growing out of an investigation that are put on record. Commonly used in the plural form (singular, datum).

common sense   Beliefs held by many people, common knowledge not necessarily based on the results of scientific study.

confounding   Having other variables enter an experiment without the knowledge of the experimenter. The effect of these variables may be to hide those of the planned independent variable, thus confounding or confusing the results.

consensus   Agreement of an informal sort reached in group decision-making.

constants   Conditions that the investigator tries to keep from varying.

controlled experiment, control   In a simple experiment, there is only one subject (or group) that gets the experimental treatment. To better judge the results, the experimenter may use what is called a control subject or group that does not get the experimental treatment but is treated in every other way like the experimental subject or group. This is called a controlled experiment.

counterbalanced experiment   Also see CONTROLLED EXPERIMENT. A controlled experiment that is done twice with the same subjects but on the second time through, the control becomes the experimental and the experimental becomes the control.

dependent variable   When the experimenter changes something to observe what happens, the things she or he changes may "cause" something else to happen. If so, the "something else" is called the dependent variable. See also INDEPENDENT VARIABLE.

empirical   Refers to the testing of a statement, question, or problem by scientific methods or other practical, real-life methods, instead of testing only by reasoning or logic.

error   In measuring, a term used to show how far apart the varying results may be. Does not mean a mistake or a wrong answer. See also STANDARD ERROR.

evaluation, evaluating results   The attempt to decide whether a science investigation has shown a satisfying or usable result, usually expressed in terms of a probability. An attempt at answering this question: Did the investigation work out to be a good test of the hypothesis?

experiment; experimental   An investigation made by changing or manipulating things (including people, on occasion) to find out what happens as a result of the changes. An experiment is usually planned to answer a specific question, to solve a problem, or to test a statement or hypothesis.

experimenter   One who plans and performs an experiment.

extrapolate   See PREDICT.

frequency distribution   A method for classifying data that is measured or counted usually with several groupings, in which the number, or frequency, of items in each group is shown.

hypothesis   In a science investigation, the hypothesis is a statement that explains what is to be tested, the purpose of the investigation, and what the investigator intends to prove or to disprove (plural, hypotheses).

independent variable   A person doing an experiment changes something to observe what happens. The "something" that he or she changes is the independent variable.

logic   Efforts to prove something by making statements or arguments.

mean or average   In statistics, the average value of a set of values. Example: Of the three values 8, 10, and 12, one finds the mean by totaling the three values (30), then dividing the total by the number of values (3), to get the mean: 10.

naturalistic observation   To observe things, animals, people, groups, and/or societies as they exist in nature.

normal distribution   A frequency distribution of a "normal" grouping. A graph of such a distribution is also sometimes called a bell curve. (See also FREQUENCY DISTRIBUTION.)

objective, objectivity   Something perceptible by all observers.

placebo   A nonacting substitute designed to be indistinguishable from a particular vitamin or medicine.

population   A large group from which a sample may be taken. In statistical work, population may refer to an unknown group that is defined only by reference to the sample at hand.

predict; extrapolate   To make judgments about a future event based on the actual observations or data at hand. To extrapolate may mean to infer about what is unknown beyond the observed range of the available data, based on data that are known.

prejudice, prejudgment   An opinion, attitude, or belief based on feelings instead of fact and held in spite of evidence for a different point of view or with no valid evidence at all. In fact, prejudice may be based on beliefs that are contrary to the evidence.

probable error   A regular difference from a mean or average.

random, randomize, random choice   One makes a random decision when the choice is made depending on the toss of a coin, the roll of dice, pulling of names out of a hat, drawing a card out of a well-shuffled deck, using a table of random numbers, or similar acts.

range   In statistical work, the difference between the highest and the lowest numbers in a series of measurements of quantities. For example, the range of ages in a group was from a four-month-old baby to a ninety-three-year-old grandmother.

reaction time   The amount of time a person or an animal takes to do a certain thing after being given a special signal. (Also called response time.)

replicate   To repeat an experiment, survey, or other investigation that is identical to the original to help determine the validity of the original.

sample   Used in statistical work with a meaning roughly equal to the common usage but also referring to highly developed methods for assuring that a sample reasonably represents the larger population from which it is taken.

scientific method   The detailed observation of things that really exist, such as events or people, in order to test hypotheses as opposed to the use of reasoning or logic alone. Empirical testing or observation.

significant difference   In an experiment or survey, the use of statistical methods to show that a certain result or difference in data occurred at a higher rate than could be expected by simple chance or accident.

standard error   A mathematical term used in statistics to express the deviation of measures from a mean or average.

statistics; statistical treatment   The rearrangement and analysis of data or factual material in an effort to get more meaning or information from the data.

subject   In an experiment or other investigation, the person, animal, or other thing the experimenter observes for the purpose of the study.

survey   An investigation of things as they currently exist to gain information or to test a hypothesis, one in which there is little or no intention to change the situation being observed.

theory   In the sciences, a newly evolved meaning of the term is to offer a causal explanation that has been tested. Also used occasionally for a causal explanation that has not been tested.

variability   A statistical term expressing for a group of values the amount of variation around the mean of those values. Thus, a set of values may have the same mean and range as another set but have greater or lesser variability. The most widely used mathematical expression of variability is called standard deviation.

variable   In a thing or pattern of things being observed, a change in a dimension or a characteristic; a change in value or quantity. See also INDEPENDENT VARIABLE and DEPENDENT VARIABLE.

BIBLIOGRAPHY

Many books have been published on the design of experiments and of surveys, on scientific methods, on statistics, and on the philosophy of science. Listed here are a few that may be useful. These I suggest primarily for science teachers and others who are helping students with science projects for science fairs. Be aware that this is a limited selection from a very large literature about how science and mathematics work.

Butterfield, Herbert. *Origins of Modern Science.* 1992. Free Press.

Chalmers, A. F. *What Is This Thing Called Science?* 1999. Open University Press.

Cohen, I. Bernard. *Revolution in Science.* 1985. Harvard University Press.

Cromer, Alan. *Uncommon Sense: The Heretical Nature of Science.* 1993. Oxford University Press.

Einstein, Albert, and Leopold Infeld. *The Evolution of Physics.* 1967. Simon and Schuster.

Galilei, Galileo. *Dialogues concerning Two New Sciences.* First published in 1638. Dover.

Gould, Stephen Jay. *An Urchin in the Storm.* 1988. Norton.

Holton, Gerald. *Science and Anti-Science.* 1993. Harvard University Press.

Keller, Evelyn Fox. *Reflections on Gender and Science.* 1985. Yale University Press.

Kitcher, Philip. *The Nature of Mathematical Knowledge.* 1983. Oxford University Press.

Klemke, E. D., et al., editors. *Introductory Readings in the Philosophy of Science.* 1988. Prometheus.

Koestler, Arthur. *The Sleepwalkers.* 1963. Viking.

Phillips, D. C. Philosophy, *Science, and Social Inquiry.* 1987. Pergamon.

Popper, Karl R. *The Logic of Scientific Discovery.* 1968. Harper.

INDEX

Note: Pages with graphs and figures are given in *italics*.